INSIDE THE
DEPARTMENT OF
Energy

Jennifer Peters

Enslow Publishing
101 W. 23rd Street
Suite 240
New York, NY 10011
USA
enslow.com

Published in 2019 by Enslow Publishing, LLC
101 W. 23rd Street, Suite 240, New York, NY 10011

Library of Congress Cataloging-in-Publication Data

Names: Peters, Jennifer, author. | Margulies, Phillip, author.
Title: Inside the Department of Energy / Jennifer Peters, Phillip Margulies.
Description: New York : Enslow Publishing, [2019] | Series: Understanding the executive branch | Includes bibliographical references and index. |Audience: Grades 5-8.
Identifiers: LCCN 2017058410| ISBN 9780766098909 (library bound) | ISBN 9780766098916 (pbk.)
Subjects: LCSH: United States. Department of Energy—Juvenile literature. | Energy policy—United States—Juvenile literature.
Classification: LCC HD9502.U52 P48 2019 | DDC 333.790973—dc23
LC record available at https://lccn.loc.gov/2017058410

Printed in the United States of America

To Our Readers: We have done our best to make sure all website addresses in this book were active and appropriate when we went to press. However, the author and the publisher have no control over and assume no liability for the material available on those websites or on any websites they may link to. Any comments or suggestions can be sent by email to customerservice@ enslow.com.

Portions of this book originally appeared in *This Is Your Government: The Department of Energy* by Phillip Margulies.

Photo Credits: Cover, p. 1 Alberto Masnovo/Shutterstock.com; pp. 5, 17, 32 Bloomberg/Getty Images; p. 8 Bill Pierce/The LIFE Images Collection/Getty Images; p. 9 Tim Wright/Corbis Documentary/Getty Images; pp. 11, 34 Scott Olson/Getty Images; p. 12 13Smile/Shutterstock. com; p. 18 George D. Lepp/Corbis Documentary/Getty Images; p. 21 Dirck Halstead/The LIFE Images Collection/Getty Images; p. 23 Herb Swanson/AFP/Getty Images; p. 27 Chip Somodevilla/Getty Images; p. 28 Justin Merriman/Getty Images; p. 30 William Campbell/ Corbis Documentary/Getty Images; p. 35 FUN FUN PHOTO/Shutterstock.com; p. 36 Igor Kostin/Sygma/Getty Images.

CONTENTS

INTRODUCTION

Every single day we use energy of one kind or another. The alarm clocks that wake us up use electricity. The cell phones we rely on to stay in touch use batteries. The cars we drive to get back and forth use gasoline. We use wind, water, and solar power to create electricity to power our homes and all the devices within them. And the businesses we rely on to provide our food, clothes—everything—rely on that same energy to operate their stores.

We depend on the gizmos and gadgets we use to do so many things, but we also rely on bigger machines, too. We count on gasoline to keep the cars on the highway moving, because if there's not enough gas and cars can't go, everyone will get stuck. We count on battery power and electricity to power the satellites that provide our cell phone service and bounce the radio television signals to our homes. We even rely on nuclear power as a source of electricity and nuclear weapons to keep us safe from war.

So much of what we do and the items we use require energy. Even small reductions in our energy supply can have huge consequences. We know this because in the 1970s, the United States experienced a shortage of gasoline. It was then that the Department of Energy (DOE) was founded.

Energy is essential for manufacturing and using the machines we rely upon.

It is the job of the Department of Energy to see to it that the country obtains the energy it needs at a cost Americans can afford. Since energy and energy policy are so vital to the prosperity and security of the United States, the Department of Energy is a cabinet-level department. This means that the person in charge of the department—the secretary of energy—is one of the president's key advisors. The secretary of energy is appointed by the president with the advice and consent of Congress— that is, a majority of senators and representatives must vote in favor of the appointment. As the head of a department with an annual budget of $32 billion, the secretary of energy possesses an enormous amount of political power and influence.

Energy policy is a complicated business because energy comes from many sources. Each energy source has its advantages and disadvantages. Energy is also very big business. Each piece of legislation relating to energy policy can represent billions of dollars of profit to some energy companies. Energy is also controversial. Some forms of energy, like coal and gasoline, can be dangerous because of how they pollute the environment, but they are also plentiful and easy to use. Other forms of energy, like solar power and wind power, are much safer, but they are harder to harness and require billions of dollars in investment up front if we want to use them later.

There are many issues that affect our energy decisions and the ways we choose and use various forms of energy. It's critical to think about how the government controls our energy usage, in both good and bad ways.

CHAPTER 1

OPENING THE CABINET TO ENERGY

The Department of Energy first became a cabinet department in 1977, at a time when American energy policy seemed incredibly important. At the time, the Middle East was exporting less oil than usual, and that meant there was less fuel for Americans. The price of fuel went up, while the amount available dropped. Soon, Americans were paying more than ever before to heat their homes and fill the gas tanks in their cars—and that was if they could get fuel in the first place. Many parts of the United States experienced gas shortages in the 1970s, and fuel was rationed, or sold in only small quantities. High energy costs were bad for businesses, so businesses hired fewer people. With high prices and high unemployment rates—all relating to the energy crisis—Americans had a lot to complain about in the 1970s, though the situation was by no means a new one.

An oil embargo spurred a nationwide gas shortage in the 1970s, leading to the founding of the Department of Energy.

KEEPING THE NATION RUNNING

To understand how the energy crisis of the 1970s came about and led to the creation of the DOE, it helps to look at the history of energy in the United States. At the time of the country's founding, energy needs were low and energy was plentiful. Americans heated their homes with firewood. For light after dark, they used candles and oil-burning lamps. Horses provided transportation. Waterpower from the flow of streams and rivers helped to grind grain into flour and run the machines of the first textile factories. The young country possessed these traditional energy sources in abundance. When mechanized industries—with their enormous energy requirements—began to grow in the United States, new energy sources such as coal and oil had to be tapped. Luckily, America was well supplied with these fossil fuels.

At the beginning of the twentieth century, the first automobiles were introduced and ran on gasoline derived from oil. America quickly became a nation of motorists, and oil replaced coal as the most important fuel source for both transportation and industry.

THE NUCLEAR AGE

Nuclear energy was first developed for use in weapons rather than as an inexpensive source of almost limitless energy. By the beginning of World War II, discoveries in physics had made it possible to create a type of bomb so powerful that it could destroy an entire city. The bomb's power would come from unleashing the force that holds the nuclei (the

While nuclear power is a cheap source of energy, nuclear waste remains radioactive for thousands of years, making it difficult to dispose of safely.

central mass) of atoms together. The energy released by breaking apart these nuclei is known as nuclear energy.

As terrifying as the destructive force of the atomic bomb was, it was argued that nuclear power could supply the nation with a limitless source of cheap energy. In 1947, Congress created the Atomic Energy Commission (AEC) to regulate both the dread and the dream of nuclear power. The AEC controlled the new arsenal of nuclear weapons the United States was creating while at the same time encouraging the development of the nuclear power industry.

In the years that followed the creation of the AEC, safe nuclear power turned out to be a lot more difficult to develop than it had at first appeared. Throughout the 1950s and 1960s, the promised golden age of unlimited power remained out of reach.

A LOOMING CRISIS

Throughout the twentieth century, as Americans came to rely more and more on cars and America's farms and factories became increasingly mechanized, the country's consumption of energy grew rapidly. By the 1960s, the United States was using more energy than any other country in the world and far more than it could produce. Very few people worried about this growing dependence on foreign energy sources, however. America was rich enough to buy all the extra energy it needed.

WHERE'S THE OIL?

The average US citizen's ideas about energy began to change in November 1973, with the beginning of the Arab oil embargo. The biggest oil producers in the world, mostly Arabic-speaking countries in

The energy crisis of the 1970s led to rationing of fuel and higher costs for the fuel that was available.

the Middle East, had become organized in two international cartels (groups of producers that have a monopoly or near monopoly on what they make). The first was called OPEC (the Organization of Petroleum Exporting Countries, which included non-Arab countries such as Iran and Venezuela). The second cartel was a smaller, all-Arab group within OPEC called OAPEC (the Organization of Arab Petroleum Exporting Countries). Having no competition, a cartel can set whatever prices it wants on its product without having to worry about competitors setting lower prices. The member countries of OAPEC and OPEC produced so much of the world's oil that they could do just that.

The event that finally unified the cartels was the victory of Israel over Syria and Egypt in the 1973 Yom Kippur War. Though the United States did not actively participate in that war, it supplied Israel with weapons and money. OAPEC decided to punish the United States for its support of Israel by refusing to ship crude oil to the United States. This became known as the Arab oil embargo.

The embargo did not eliminate America's access to oil. America still produced some of its own oil, and not all petroleum-exporting countries took part in the embargo. But the Arab oil embargo did create shortages and raised the price of energy. The most visible signs of the shortage

Since oil is a widely used resource that can't be replaced, it is extremely valuable. In 1973, the OAPEC cartel refused to ship oil to the United States, driving up gas and oil prices.

were around-the-block lines at gas stations all over the country and very high prices for heating oil.

WHAT COMES NEXT?

When the Arab oil embargo ended, in March of 1974, the gas lines disappeared and so, at first, did the feeling that there was an energy "crisis." Oil prices remained high, however. Through the actions of OAPEC members, OPEC, the larger cartel, became aware of its strength. OPEC members realized that even if they could not use their near-monopoly on oil to affect US foreign policy, they could work together to get a better price for each barrel of oil they sold. Due to OPEC's cutting of oil production, gas prices remained high all over the world long after the embargo ended.

The presidential administrations of Gerald Ford (1974–1977) and Jimmy Carter (1977–1981) continued to try to develop a national energy policy. Plans were made to explore new oil reserves in Alaska and to further develop nuclear energy in the United States. Americans began to debate the solutions to the energy problem. Should gasoline be taxed to encourage Americans to conserve energy? Should nuclear power be developed, despite its dangers? Should alternative energy sources, such as solar power, be explored?

Even as Americans became aware of the problems caused by high energy prices, more and more people were also concerned about the environmental problems caused by the most commonly used energy sources. Coal mining damaged the landscape. Burning both coal and oil added to air pollution. Nuclear power created dangerous radioactive

PREVENTING FUTURE OIL SHORTAGES

For decades, many American politicians and Energy Department officials have recognized the importance of setting aside a supply of oil within the United States in case of emergency shortages of foreign oil. The 1973–74 oil embargo finally made the government commit to an oil reserve. In the aftermath of the oil crisis, the United States established the Strategic Petroleum Reserve (SPR). President Gerald Ford created the SPR when he signed the Energy Policy and Conservation Act on December 22, 1975. From then on, oil owned by the federal government would be stored in huge underground salt caverns along the coastline of the Gulf of Mexico. These caverns have the capacity to hold 727 million barrels. It is the largest emergency oil stockpile in the world.

waste products and the potential for disastrous nuclear accidents. Regulations that would make energy production less harmful to the environment would drive up the cost of energy. Americans wanted a healthy environment, but they also wanted cheap energy. How could both these desires be met?

While successfully campaigning against President Gerald Ford in 1976, Jimmy Carter promised to create a cabinet-level Department of Energy to address these questions and seek solutions. Soon after his inauguration, Carter appointed James R. Schlesinger to study the energy problem and present a comprehensive plan to Congress.

On February 2, 1977, Carter addressed the nation in a fireside chat, stressing the need for conservation to solve the energy problem. In April, sending his energy legislation to Congress, Carter described the energy crisis as "the moral equivalent to war." On August 4, 1977, Carter signed the bill that created the Department of Energy, and Schlesinger became its first secretary.

CHAPTER 2

LEADING THE DEPARTMENT OF ENERGY

Secretaries of energy, like all cabinet members, work to carry out the wishes of the president who appointed them. The policies of the various secretaries of energy have always tended to reflect the aims of the president in office at the time. These aims have varied greatly, depending on what party the president belonged to, as well as the country's changing energy needs.

JAMES SCHLESINGER AND OIL CONSERVATION

James R. Schlesinger was the first and most influential secretary of energy. Schlesinger helped to draft the law that created the DOE and formulated the country's basic strategies for dealing with the energy crisis of the 1970s.

Before he became secretary of the Energy Department, he had at different times been chairman of the Atomic Energy Commission, director of the Central Intelligence Agency (the CIA, America's spy network), and the secretary of the Defense Department. Carter relied on Schlesinger to help him create his energy plan and design the DOE. Schlesinger even helped write the proposals outlining the DOE's responsibilities that would be sent to Congress for approval.

To encourage conservation of oil, Schlesinger wanted to place a tax on it. Very few Americans wanted to pay more for gasoline, even if it was supposed to be good medicine for the economy and the environment. Sensing the voters' disapproval, Congress rejected the deregulation and tax portions of the Carter administration's energy plan. Carter said that his original proposals would have lowered oil imports by an estimated 4.5 million barrels per day by 1985. In its final form, the new legislation would save 2.5 million barrels per day.

Aside from Carter's controversial and sweeping energy policy, two other incidents occurred while Schlesinger was in office that had long-term effects on American energy policy and the work of the secretary of energy—the Iranian Revolution and the crisis at the Three Mile Island nuclear power plant.

ANOTHER ENERGY CRISIS

On January 16, 1979, there was a revolution in Iran, a major oil-exporting country. The country's leader, Shah Mohammad Reza Pahlavi, an American ally, was forced to flee the country. The new Iranian regime stopped exporting oil and soon created a worldwide shortage. Other

President Trump's secretary of energy, Rick Perry, has pushed for greater investment in coal and nuclear energy.

oil-exporting nations took advantage of the shortage and raised their prices. Carter called on the United States to voluntarily conserve energy until normal oil supplies were again available.

Once again there were lines around the block to fill tanks at gas stations and fuel prices skyrocketed. In order to control fuel use and reduce the gas lines, drivers were only allowed to buy gas on alternate days. Their fill-up days were assigned based on whether their license plates ended with an odd or even number. President Carter delivered another speech on the crisis and energy policy. He outlined a very detailed and complex policy that combined more energy production, more conservation, and the use of subsidies to help develop alternatives to energy. Together, these proposals were meant to cut energy use and reduce dependence on foreign suppliers.

NUCLEAR DISASTER

On March 28, 1979, in the midst of the energy crisis, the United States experienced a major nuclear accident. In the early hours of that Wednesday morning, two water pumps in the cooling system at Three Mile Island (TMI), a large nuclear power plant in the small town of Harrisburg, Pennsylvania, stopped operating. A series of errors quickly resulted in the worst nuclear accident in US history.

Three Mile Island is the site of the most serious nuclear power accident in US history. Though no one was harmed, some radioactive gases were released into the atmosphere.

Had the situation not been brought under control in time, it might have led to the worst of all possible human-made disasters: total nuclear meltdown. Thankfully, no one was killed or even injured as a result of the Three Mile Island disaster. It did leave the power plant inoperable, however, and cost nearly $1 billion to clean up. More important, it had a serious and lasting effect on American nuclear energy policy and development.

CONTAINING NUCLEAR FALLOUT

The Office of Civilian Radioactive Waste Management (CRWM) is a program administered by the Department of Energy. Its job is to develop and manage a nationwide system for disposing of spent nuclear fuel from commercial nuclear reactors and high-level radioactive waste from national defense activities, such as weapons production and the construction of nuclear-powered submarines. Most nuclear waste—as much as 90 percent—is fairly safe and can be disposed of easily. The other 10 percent, however, is very dangerous, and the CRWM is responsible for making sure that waste is disposed of properly so that it doesn't lead to environmental issues or cause citizens living near the disposal sites to be exposed to unsafe levels of radiation.

The disaster at the plant changed the way that the public viewed nuclear energy. People became far more skeptical of the limitless and "safe" uses of nuclear fuel. Not a single new nuclear power plant has been ordered in the United States since the accident at Three Mile Island. In order to address the public's fears and concerns, the Nuclear Regulatory Commission was forced to change and strengthen the ways in which nuclear power plants are operated.

HOW MUCH GOVERNMENT HELP DO WE NEED?

During his 1980 presidential campaign, Ronald Reagan promised to abolish the Department of Energy. Americans should rely on private enterprise—not the government—to solve the country's energy problems, Reagan said. Soon after taking office, President Reagan selected

James B. Edwards, the governor of South Carolina, as the nation's third secretary of energy. As energy secretary, Edwards argued for a more limited government role in setting energy policy. Edwards believed that free enterprise could solve most energy problems. Since many of the United States' natural energy resources—its reserves of coal, oil, and natural gas—were controlled by the government, the best thing the government could do to help reduce America's dependence on foreign oil would be to give American companies easy access to these resources. Edwards also wanted to encourage the further development of nuclear energy by making it easier for companies to get licenses to open and operate nuclear energy plants.

Reagan and Edwards pushed plans to let private companies develop the energy resources under government control (such as much of the country's coal and oil shale). In line with Reagan's campaign promise, Edwards hoped to be able to dismantle the Department of Energy as a cabinet-level department. He planned to fold it into another agency, such as the Department of Commerce, but Congress did not allow it.

JAMES D. WATKINS

Soon after George H. W. Bush was elected president in 1988, he picked James D. Watkins, a former chief of naval operations for the US Navy with training as a nuclear engineer, to be his secretary of energy. Watkins, a conservative Republican, agreed with Bush that it was best to let the free market determine prices for energy, especially for coal, oil, and natural gas. Watkins was a strong supporter of nuclear energy, but

Energy secretary James Watkins (*far right*) believed businesses should set the prices for energy like coal or oil, not the government.

he was also worried about the problem of what to do with the radioactive waste that was a by-product of nuclear energy production.

Two important events related to energy policy and use occurred during Watkins's tenure as secretary of energy. The first of these was the 1990 Gulf War, which followed Iraqi president Saddam Hussein's invasion of Kuwait, a small neighboring country. Saddam hoped to gain control of Kuwait's valuable oil fields. With the agreement of the United Nations, the United States and a multinational armed force drove Saddam out of Kuwait. Meanwhile, Secretary Watkins announced plans to increase oil production and decrease consumption to counteract the expected temporary loss of

Iraqi and Kuwaiti oil. Oil production was not seriously interrupted, however, and oil prices remained relatively low throughout the 1990s.

A second energy-related crisis that occurred early in Bush's presidency was the 1989 *Exxon Valdez* oil spill. The *Exxon Valdez* was a giant oil tanker that carried crude oil from a pipeline in Alaska. It ran aground soon after it had picked up its cargo. Almost 11 million gallons (41.6 million liters) of oil spilled into Prince William Sound, creating a slick that covered 1,000 square miles (2,590 square kilometers). Scientists believe that 40 percent of the 11 million gallons was eventually washed up on beaches, 35 percent of it evaporated, and 25 percent entered the Gulf of Alaska and either washed ashore or was carried out to sea.

In the wake of the *Exxon Valdez* accident, Congress passed the Oil Pollution Act in 1990. This new law ordered changes to be made that would help prevent future oil spills and reduce damage to the environment when spills occurred. Public attention was once more drawn to the difficulty of reconciling energy use with protection of the environment. After the accident, many Americans began to view the oil industry as a profit-obsessed, irresponsible enemy of the environment.

THE DEMOCRATS GET CONTROL OF ENERGY AGAIN

During his successful presidential campaign in 1992, Bill Clinton said the Bush and Reagan administrations' energy policies had been too influenced by the big oil companies. He promised to break their hold on energy policy and instead emphasize conservation and fuel efficiency. Clinton and his vice president, Al Gore, were both strong supporters of pro-environment energy regulation and promised to develop energy policies that would promote the use of renewable resources (like wind and solar power that can not be used up like fossil fuels). Clinton's three secretaries of energy—Hazel O'Leary (1993–1997), Federico Pena (1997–1998), and Bill Richardson (1998–2001)—worked to carry out this policy.

The pro-environment aims of Clinton's secretaries of energy were frustrated by one important trend: oil was abundant and relatively cheap throughout the 1990s. Despite the Clinton administration's attempts to encourage conservation, most Americans did not feel that the nation was in the midst of an energy crisis.

In 1993, Hazel O'Leary became the first woman and the first person of color to be appointed as secretary of energy.

ENERGY EXECUTIVES IN THE WHITE HOUSE

George W. Bush (the son of George H. W. Bush) became president in 2000. He and his vice president, Dick Cheney, were both former oil company executives. During his presidential campaign, Bush criticized the Clinton administration's pro-environment energy policies. Bush argued that the development of America's oil reserves was vitally important to the creation of a more abundant supply of energy and decreased American dependence on foreign oil at a time of great political instability in the oil-rich Middle East.

As promised during Bush's campaign, his secretary of energy, Spencer Abraham, pursued policies intended to loosen the environmental regulations that had prevented some of the nation's most delicate, beautiful, and protected public lands from being made available for drilling and logging.

LEADING THE CHARGE FOR RENEWABLE ENERGY

After taking office in 2008, President Barack Obama immediately set to work to encourage the United States to take energy conservation seriously once again. With the help of his energy secretaries, Steven Chu and Ernest Moniz, Obama worked to push for renewable energy, such as wind, solar, and hydro (water) power. He also prevented energy companies from doing offshore drilling in the Arctic, preserving the polar region from potential drilling accidents, and prohibited the creation of the Keystone XL and Dakota Access Pipelines to prevent damage to the environment. At the same time, Obama's administration more heavily regulated the fossil fuel industries, creating strict new rules for coal and oil companies.

UNDOING OBAMA'S LEGACY

Following his surprise election in 2016, President Donald Trump immediately set about undoing much of the Obama administration's work. Just days after taking office, Trump signed two executive orders that would make way for the Keystone XL and Dakota Access Pipelines to be expanded and constructed. He then appointed Rick Perry as his secretary of energy—even though Perry once famously forgot that the Department of Energy even existed.

Ten months into Trump's presidency, the Keystone Pipeline experienced an oil spill in South Dakota, with more than 200,000 barrels of oil leaking from the pipeline. Although no livestock or humans were immediately impacted by the spill, it proved that the pipeline wasn't as safe as the president believed and that expansion of the pipeline could lead to further, more damaging accidents.

CHAPTER 3

WHAT DOES THE DEPARTMENT OF ENERGY DO?

The primary job of the United States secretary of energy is to advise the president on energy policy and to help make sure the United States has enough energy to meet its needs. Because energy is crucial to so much of American life, the activities of the Department of Energy have a bigger impact on citizens' lives than most people generally realize.

The Department of Energy must concern itself with matters as different as assuring that electric companies charge their customers a fair price to ensuring that radioactivity from nuclear waste does not leak into groundwater and endanger the health of residents who live nearby. The leadership of the Department of Energy is responsible for the operation of a $32 billion organization that employs more than 115,000 people.

Under the Obama administration, the Department of Energy focused on developing energy sources that could be replaced easily, like solar power.

FOLLOWING THE MISSION

There are so many different agencies within the Department of Energy that it would take a quite a long time to describe all of them. However, the DOE's activities can be boiled down to four basic "mission areas," which are the four main jobs that the department is responsible for: national security, energy resources, science and technology, and environmental quality.

ENERGY RESOURCES

The Department of Energy must see to it that there is enough energy—whether in the form of oil, gas, coal, nuclear, water, wind, or solar—to meet

Coal use has declined in recent years as the United States seeks better sources of energy, leaving many coal miners without work.

the country's needs. Through the Federal Energy Regulatory Commission (FERC), the Department of Energy regulates the sale of energy to businesses and homes. It works to keep electricity prices fair, licenses hydro-electric dams (which convert the energy of rushing water into electricity), regulates the transportation of petroleum products, and grants permission to the companies that want to operate interstate natural gas facilities.

NATIONAL SECURITY

Through the National Nuclear Security Administration (NNSA), the Department of Energy regulates and keeps track of nuclear energy. It develops nuclear weapons, keeps them in working order, and ensures their safekeeping. In addition, the NNSA encourages nuclear nonprolifera-tion. "Nonproliferation" means not letting something spread or grow. Nuclear nonproliferation activities involve working to see that countries that do not have nuclear weapons do not develop or obtain them and that countries that do have them do not sell them to nonnuclear countries or individuals. The greater the number of countries that have nuclear weapons, the greater the danger that there will be a deadly nuclear attack or accident.

THE WEIRD WORLD OF ENERGY RESEARCH

Every year, the Advanced Research Projects Agency–Energy (ARPA–E) gives scientists grants to do special research into weird and wild new ideas for the American energy sector. It funds crazy-sounding research in hopes of inspiring scientists to think outside the box and find new ways to improve the ways Americans get and use energy. Among some of the most unique ideas to come from these special grants are: ways to harness energy from swirling dust storms; batteries that run on air; growing diamonds to be used as electric conductors; and tapping pine trees to create a new biofuel. Though they seem like long shots, ARPA–E hopes that they will lead to helpful new discoveries.

ENVIRONMENTAL QUALITY

All forms of energy production and consumption have major effects on the environment. The burning of coal, oil, and gas adds to air pollution. Mining coal can wreck the landscape. Oil spills kill ocean and shore wildlife. Generating nuclear power creates cancer-causing nuclear waste products that can end up in our streams, air, and soil and remain poisonous for thousands of years. Even hydroelectric dams and windmills cause some harm to wildlife. Since the production, distribution, and consumption of energy all have powerful effects on the environment, environmental quality is a major concern of the DOE's Office of Environmental Management (EM).

RESEARCH

The Department of Energy employs or funds scientists to undertake its research projects. Some of this research is aimed at developing new ways of generating and distributing energy, such as research into solar energy and the development of hydrogen-powered electric cars. Other projects have nothing to do with the nation's energy needs but draw on technol-

Like solar energy, the energy drawn from wind is easily replaceable. A collection of over a hundred wind turbines can provide power for tens of thousands of homes.

ogies that were originally developed by the nuclear energy industry. For example, the Department of Energy has a medical sciences division, which does basic research in scientific fields like nuclear medicine. Nuclear medicine uses very small amounts of radioactive materials to diagnose and treat disease.

Nuclear medicine can be used to perform stress tests on the heart, scan bones to identify injuries, and scan lungs for blood clots, among many other things.

CHAPTER 4

TODAY'S DEPARTMENT OF ENERGY

Through its policies and practices, the Department of Energy must answer questions about how Americans and the US government should produce and use energy. It must consider whether the United States should continue to use as much energy as it's currently using, whether it should drill for oil within its own borders or rely on other countries to provide its fuel, and whether renewable energy is worth investing in now or if the country can continue to rely on fossil fuels.

Developing an energy policy that tackles these questions and tries to answer them with concrete actions will almost certainly favor either industry or the environment. Striking a balance between the needs of both will be extremely difficult. Whichever direction the DOE chooses, the consequences of its energy policy will have a profound impact on the way we live in the twenty-first century.

Stepping back from President Obama's investment in alternative energy sources like solar and wind power, President Trump wants the United States to finance coal-fired power plants.

LOOKING TO THE FUTURE

Three particular energy problems and proposed solutions that are currently being debated give an idea of the problems that will be faced by future secretaries of energy.

NUCLEAR WASTE DISPOSAL

For more than fifteen years, America has been debating the construction of a nuclear waste repository (storage facility) deep inside a mountain in the Nevada desert. The site, officially known as the Yucca Mountain Nuclear Waste Repository, is located 1,000 feet (305 meters) below Yucca Mountain, 90 miles (145 km) from the city of Las Vegas. If the repository is ever completed, it would accept more than 77,000 tons (69,853 tonnes) of nuclear waste.

Nuclear waste is produced by the power plants that generate nuclear energy and also by the manufacture of nuclear weapons. When human beings are exposed to nuclear waste in large quantities, they get radiation poisoning and usually die quickly. When they are exposed to smaller quantities of radiation, they suffer an increased risk of cancer and birth defects. There is no way to turn nuclear waste into something harmless. Its radioactivity cannot be removed and destroyed. Instead, it must break down on its own over thousands of years. Radioactive materials can only be contained during this long period, and this is not easy to do.

There are many questions about the safety of the Yucca Mountain repository. Some say that over time radioactive materials stored in the earth will seep into groundwater and then enter nearby rivers, streams, and lakes, eventually finding their way to large population centers. Others point to the danger posed by regularly scheduled deliveries of nuclear waste to a single site in Nevada.

KEEPING AMERICA CLEAN

The DOE's Environmental Management (EM) program is responsible for cleaning up the soil and water at and around its former nuclear weapons sites. EM cleans up soil using a variety of methods. Sometimes it removes the contaminated soil and stores it in a special facility designed to hold contaminants. Other contaminants can be removed at the site, leaving the soil in place. Occasionally, natural remedies can be used to clean up a site, such as the planting of certain kinds of vegetation that can soak up contaminants. To clean up contaminated surface water and groundwater, the EM can simply pump the water out of the ground, remove the contaminant, and pump the water back into the ground. Cleaned-up land and water sites are then monitored by the EM for years to ensure that no further contamination occurs.

Safe storage and disposal of nuclear waste is a major challenge because of the contamination risk of the radioactive material seeping into groundwater.

The problems of nuclear waste disposal and storage will continue to be a troubling issue for future secretaries of energy.

POLLUTION-FREE FUEL

In his January, 28, 2003, State of the Union address, President George W. Bush proposed a $1.2 billion research project with the aim of developing clean, hydrogen-powered automobiles. The president noted that a relatively simple chemical reaction between hydrogen and oxygen can generate enough energy to power cars. These hydrogen-powered cars would not contribute to air pollution because the only waste they would produce is water, not exhaust fumes.

This form of energy discussed by President Bush does seem to have an exciting future. Oxygen and hydrogen are currently being combined to generate electricity in the form of fuel cells. Cars may one day contain fuel cells instead of gas tanks. Many obstacles lie in the path of this invention, however.

The chief obstacle is that, in the case of hydrogen fuel cells, it takes energy to make energy. In fact, a lot more energy is spent obtaining the hydrogen for fuel cells than is actually made by those cells when hydrogen and oxygen are combined to generate electricity. Separating the hydrogen from other elements uses energy, making hydrogen impractical as a major source of power.

Though cars powered by hydrogen aren't practical, electric cars are becoming more popular.

The accident at the Chernobyl power plant in Ukraine was an example of the dangers of nuclear power, causing cancer and other health problems for people nearby.

THE RUSSIAN NUKE QUESTION

The arms race between the Soviet Union and the United States, which lasted from the late 1940s to the late 1980s, was a central part of the Cold War. The Cold War was a decades-long nonmilitary conflict between the two superpowers. The source of this simmering tension was the nations' political differences. The United States promoted democracy while the Soviet Union supported Communism. While opposing each other, both countries tried to gain influence with the other nations of the world. During the Cold War, each side built enough nuclear bombs to destroy all life on this planet many times over.

Then, in the early 1990s, the Communist dictatorship that had dominated the Soviet Union collapsed. The new, weaker Russia was no longer hostile to the United States and was eager to engage in treaties with the United States to reduce the number of nuclear weapons in both countries.

To deal with the leftover nukes, in the 1990s the DOE developed programs meant to help Russia track and dispose of its nuclear weapons, convert the Russian nuclear weapons program to peaceful (power-generating) uses, and find civilian (nonmilitary) employment within Russia for its nuclear scientists.

The danger posed by the often unsecured and poorly guarded nuclear materials spread throughout the former Soviet Union will haunt the secretaries of energy for many years to come.

CONCLUSION

As America moves further into the twenty-first century and relies more and more on machines, computers, and digital devices to go about its everyday business, the country will require more and more energy. Where that energy comes from and how Americans use it will be under the jurisdiction of the Department of Energy.

To keep up with the needs of the country, the secretary of energy will need to figure out how to produce more energy and what energy sources to use. He or she will need to weigh the energy needs of America's citizens against the consequences of each energy source. And it will be up to Americans like you to decide how much energy you need and what you're willing to accept to continue to use more energy. Are you willing to accept the dangers of nuclear energy if it means having an endless supply of electricity? Do you want to incur the costs of renewable energy now if it means cheaper energy costs down the line? Will you give up driving your car to walk more or take the bus if it means protecting the environment from pollution created by fossil fuels?

These questions and more will need to be answered as we face the energy challenges presented by the technological advances of the twenty-first century, and the secretary of energy will be the one guiding us to the answers.

CHRONOLOGY

1954 President Dwight D. Eisenhower signs the Atomic Energy Act of 1954, opening the way for development of a civilian nuclear power program.

October 1973 The Yom Kippur War breaks out in the Middle East. On October 17, 1973, the Organization of Arab Petroleum Exporting Countries declares an oil embargo, sparking the first energy crisis in the United States.

1975 President Gerald R. Ford signs the Energy Policy and Conservation Act, extending oil price controls into 1979, mandating automobile fuel economy standards, and authorizing creation of a strategic petroleum reserve.

1977 President Jimmy Carter announces the National Energy Plan in his first major energy speech. His plan calls for the establishment of the cabinet-level Department of Energy. James Schlesinger is appointed the first secretary of energy.

January 1979 The shah flees Iran. A cessation of oil exports results in a worldwide shortage of oil. Oil-consuming nations are using two million barrels of oil more a day than are being produced.

March 1979 An accident occurs at the Three Mile Island nuclear power plant in Pennsylvania.

June 1979 President Jimmy Carter announces a program to increase the nation's use of solar energy, including increased funds for solar energy research and development.

July 1979 President Carter proclaims a national energy supply shortage and establishes temperature restrictions in nonresidential buildings.

February 1981 Secretary James B. Edwards announces a major reorganization of the DOE to improve management and increase emphasis on research, development, and production.

May 1982 President Ronald Reagan proposes legislation transferring most responsibilities of the DOE to the Department of Commerce. Congress fails to act on the proposal.

1990 Iraq invades and seizes Kuwait, creating a major international crisis. Secretary Watkins announces plans to increase oil production and decrease consumption to counter Iraqi-Kuwaiti oil losses.

October 1993 President Bill Clinton and Vice President Al Gore unveil the Climate Change Action Plan, emphasizing voluntary measures to stabilize greenhouse gas emissions.

September 1998 Secretary Bill Richardson and Russian minister of atomic energy Yevgeny Adamov sign two agreements designed to ease the transformation of Russia's nuclear arms program to commercial uses.

1999 The Department of Energy announces the Wind Powering America initiative, designed to significantly increase the use of wind power in the United States over the next ten years.

2000 The department activates the National Nuclear Security Administration (NNSA). NNSA's mission includes maintenance of a safe, secure, and reliable stockpile of nuclear weapons and associated materials, capabilities, and technologies; promotion of international nuclear safety and nonproliferation; and administration and management of the naval nuclear propulsion program.

March 2001 Secretary Spencer Abraham formally establishes the Northeast Home Heating Oil Reserve, a two-million barrel reserve of government-owned heating oil to be used in cases of extreme circumstances of weather or threat to life.

May 2001 President George W. Bush releases the National Energy Policy (NEP) developed by his energy task force, chaired by Vice President Cheney. The NEP urges actions to meet five specific goals: modernizing conservation, modernizing the energy infrastructure, increasing energy supplies, accelerating the protection and improvement of the environment, and increasing the nation's energy security.

December 2001 Senate Democrats propose an alternative energy bill that stresses conservation, efficiency, and development of new resources over expanded drilling on public land, including Alaska's Arctic National Wildlife Refuge.

2002 The Senate votes down an amendment to the energy bill that would allow drilling for oil and gas in Alaska's Arctic National Wildlife Refuge.

2007 The Advanced Research Projects Agency–Energy is created to fund research on new methods for the production and distribution of energy.

2012 The DOE awards a grant to Ames Laboratory to begin research into rare earth elements, which are key ingredients in the production of things like cell phone batteries.

2017 President Donald Trump appoints Rick Perry as secretary of defense.

GLOSSARY

Atomic Energy Commission A federal agency established in 1947 to engage in nuclear weapons development and promote the development of atomic energy. The AEC was abolished in 1975, and its responsibilities were inherited by the US Department of Energy.

bill A draft of a law presented to a legislature and submitted to a vote.

cabinet-level department A government office headed by a key advisor to a head of state, such as the president of the United States.

cartel A group of commercial producers who join forces in order to limit competition or to set prices at a certain level.

Congress The supreme legislative body of the United States, comprised of the Senate and the House of Representatives.

conservation The planned management of a natural resource to prevent its destruction or neglect.

domestically produced oil Oil produced within the borders of the United States.

embargo A cutting off of trade.

global warming A consistent and substantial rise in the average surface temperature on Earth.

greenhouse gases Gases like carbon dioxide and methane that promote global warming.

hydroelectric Relating to the production of electricity by water.

oil reserves Sources of oil on US government property, set aside for future use during energy supply emergencies.

oil spill An accident in which an oil tanker releases its cargo of crude oil into the ocean or a pipeline leaks into the ground.

Organization of Arab Petroleum Exporting Countries (OAPEC) A group of ten Arab oil-exporting countries established in 1968 to control oil pricing and production and to influence the foreign policy of oil-importing nations. All members of OAPEC are also members of OPEC, which includes some non-Arab nations.

Organization of Petroleum Exporting Countries (OPEC) A cartel of major oil-exporting countries established in 1960 to control the pricing and production of oil. In 2002, more than 77 percent of the world's proven oil reserves lay under the soil of OPEC member nations.

FURTHER READING

BOOKS

Fetter-Vorm, Jonathan. *Trinity: A Graphic History of the First Atomic Bomb*. New York, NY: Hill and Wang, 2013.

Parker, Steve. *Electricity*. New York, NY: DK Children, 2013.

Sneideman, Joshua, and Erin Twamley. *Renewable Energy: Discover the Fuel of the Future with 20 Projects*. White River Junction, VT: Nomad Press, 2017.

WEBSITES

American Museum of Science and Energy (AMSE)

www.amse.org

Run by the Department of Energy, the AMSE provides information and education on the DOE and energy in general.

United States Department of Energy

www.energy.gov

The official website of the DOE provides updates on energy policy and legislation and information on all past projects and secretaries.

BIBLIOGRAPHY

Christensen, John. *Global Science: Energy Resources Environment.* Dubuque, IA: Kendall/Hunt Publishing Company, 2000.

Crawford, Leslie. *Energy Conservation.* Parsippany, NJ: Dale Seymour Publications, 1997.

DiChristopher, Tom. "Trump Signs Executive Actions to Advance Keystone XL, Dakota Access Pipelines." CNBC.com, January 24, 2017. https://www.cnbc.com/2017/01/24/trump-to-advance-keystone-dakota-pipelines-with-executive-order-on-tuesday-nbc.html.

Fehrenbacher, Katie. "The Weird, Wacky & Cool Energy Ideas Coming Out of Labs Across the US." GigaOm, February 26, 2014. https://gigaom.com/2014/02/26/the-weird-wacky-cool-energy-ideas-coming-out-of-labs-across-the-u-s/.

Geller, Howard. *Energy Revolution: Policies for a Sustainable Future.* Washington, DC: Island Press, 2002.

Heinberg, Richard. *The Party's Over: Oil, War, and the Fate of Industrial Societies.* Gabriola Island, British Columbia: New Society, 2003.

Hoffmann, Peter. *Tomorrow's Energy: Hydrogen, Fuel Cells, and the Prospects for a Cleaner Planet.* Cambridge, MA: MIT Press, 2002.

Lanouette, William. "James D. Watkins: Frustrated Admiral of Energy." *Bulletin of the Atomic Scientists*, January/February 1990. Retrieved October 2003. http://www.thebulletin.org/issues/1990/jf90/jf90lanouette.htm.

Maloney, Peter. "Yucca Mountain: High Stakes and High Hurdles." July 21, 2017. http://www.yuccamountain.org/pdf-news/yucca_072117.pdf.

NewsMax.com. "Feds Push Fuel Cells." January 10, 2002. Retrieved October 2003. http://www.newsmax.com/archives/articles/2002/1/9/144451.shtml.

New York Times. "Rick Perry's Energy Department 'Oops' Moment." https://www.nytimes.com/video/us/politics/100000004820721/rick-perrys-energy-department-oops-moment.html.

The Osgood File. "Nuclear Terrorism." CBS Radio Network, October 22, 2001. Retrieved October 2003. http://www.acfnewsource.org/general/nuclear_terrorism.html.

Rapier, Robert. "President Obama's Energy Report Card." Forbes.com, December 12, 2016. https://www.forbes.com/sites/rrapier/2016/12/12/president-obamas-energy-report-card/#4b62f24a554e.

Smith, Mitch, and Julie Bosman. "Keystone Pipeline Leaks 210,000 Gallons of Oil in South Dakota." New York Times, November 16, 2017. https://www.nytimes.com/2017/11/16/us/keystone-pipeline-leaks-south-dakota.html.

US Department of Energy. "Institutional Origins of the U.S. Department of Energy." 2002. Retrieved October 2003. http://www.dpi.anl.gov/dpi2/instorig/instorig1.htm.

US Department of Energy. "U.S. Department of Energy: 25th Anniversary." 2002. Retrieved October 2003. http://www.25years ofenergy.gov.

Wald, Matthew L. "Doubt Cast on Prime Site as Nuclear Waste Dump." New York Times, June 20, 1997. Retrieved October 2003. http://www.state.nv.us/nucwaste/yucca/nys01.htm.

YuccaMountain.org. "FAQs." http://www.yuccamountain.org/faq.htm.

INDEX